Mum..

TODAY'S DATE:

Mum's name:

Colour or write words
MUM

YOU BECAME MY MUM IN THE YEAR:

I LOVE YOU

more than

TOP 5

things I love about you...

something you say
A LOT...

Me to you..

Something I say to you all the time!!

Some of Mum's favourite things:

Colour

Food

Drink

Animal

Flower

Book

Movie

Draw mum here:

Our favourite holiday
Year:
Where:

LIKES

DISLIKES

To my mum

I'm so glad you're mine!

Draw

a nose, mouth and hair on each pebble

YOUR
FAVOURITE
FLOWER IS:

I blooming love you

Lessons you've taught me:

Doodle page

You get **MAD** when I...

·····································

·····································

·····································

·····································

·····································

YOUR FAVOURITE DAY OF THE WEEK IS:-

because:-

4 things you're good at:

1

2

3

4

Mum's House Rules:

Lots of Love from:

I LOVE YOU

mum

[muhm] noun.

The one who's loved me unconditionally, the one who puts me before herself and the one who you can always count on, above anyone else.

You are my EVERYTHING
and I will always love you right back!

Love from:

Keepsake Publishing